T0303687

EGGS IN PURGATORY

GENANNE WALSH

Edited by Peg Alford Pursell
Designed by Kali Browne
Cover photograph courtesy of the author

Library of Congress Cataloging-in-Publication data is on file with the Library of Congress.
Walsh, Genanne.
Eggs in Purgatory / Genanne Walsh
ISBN 978-1-7329820-9-3 (pbk) | 978-1-7336619-0-4 (ebook)

Published by WTAW Press
PO Box 2825
Santa Rosa, CA 95405
www.wtawpress.org

WTAW Press is a not-for-profit literary press. We are grateful for the assistance we receive from individual donors, public arts agencies, and private foundations.

Lines from "When Death Comes," by Mary Oliver. Reprinted by the permission of The Charlotte Sheedy Literary Agency as agent for the author. Copyright © 1992, 2006, 2017 by Mary Oliver with permission of Bill Reichblum.

CALIFORNIA
ARTS COUNCIL
A STATE AGENCY

For the caregivers

and each body a lion of courage, and something precious to the earth.

—*Mary Oliver*

EGGS IN PURGATORY

I WAS WALKING TO LUNCH with coworkers on my first day in a new job when my wife called. She told me she thought my father might be trying to kill himself. She was working at home that day and noticed late in the morning that my father's curtains were still drawn. He lived in the apartment downstairs, on the first floor of our small house in San Francisco, and he'd always been an early riser. When he didn't respond to knocking, she'd let herself in. There was a letter addressed to me on the kitchen table. His bedroom door was shut, and she'd knocked but hadn't entered. Standing at the door she could hear loud snoring—he was alive, but she thought I should come home right now.

I left my new colleagues abruptly, ran to the subway, caught a train and hurtled though the dark. It felt as though I was in transit toward some new version of my life. I heard my blood in my ears.

Soon enough I was outside his bedroom door. His snoring was noisy, committed, assertively alive. But once I entered and turned on the light, I could see that milky vomit stained his blue cotton t-shirt. I shook him but he did not respond. I called, "Dad. Daddy." I said, "Dad, sweetheart"—a term of endearment so unfamiliar it must have come from some lost fold of my brain. A bottle of over-the-counter Walgreens "sleep aids" sat empty on the bedside table. I didn't know what the pills would do. I didn't know when he'd taken them. But I knew what he wanted.

My father had talked about his end for as long as I could remember—since long before he was elderly. It was one of his defining themes: the end of life should be a personal choice, and he wanted no prolonging medical procedures. No dragging it out, no loss of self-sufficiency. He admired the Hemlock Society and a group called Compassion and Choices, and he'd asserted his position even more vociferously when he'd moved to California from New York eight years before to live downstairs. He had a living will, DNR, and POLST

(Provider Orders for Life Sustaining Treatment) documents: no resuscitation, no life-prolonging medical procedures, no matter what. Though he usually kept me at arm's length when he went to the doctor, five years before he'd brought me with him so the three of us could go over the documents. He'd attached a multi-page addendum to the forms, detailing not just his thoughts about medical care but the spiritual convictions at the root: "My objective is based on my own personal understanding that so-called "end of life" or death pertains to my body, not my spirit." He believed he was part of a universal consciousness and would continue—embodied or not—and demanded the medical establishment step out of the way. He'd made sure his doctor and I both had photocopies of his wishes, handwritten on a legal pad in numbered outline form, key words underlined or all in caps. An idiosyncratic manifesto, completely and utterly him.

So I knew what to do in the event of a heart attack or a crippling bout of pneumonia. But not with this. Not a suicide attempt.

Until that day, how to handle his *non*-life-threatening medical needs was the main point of conflict between us. He was stubborn, regularly refusing to address what seemed to be readily treatable issues. Once, trying to convince him to make an appointment to have a doctor look at an alarming mole on his temple, I'd cautioned, "Skin cancer is a terrible way to die." This did not convince him to seek a medical opinion.

"Whatever happens," he'd said, "No hospitalization. I won't prolong the end."

"But what if you fall and break a hip or an arm?" I countered. "What if you just can't care for yourself and need help?"

His eyes blazed. "Carry me to bed and leave me there." He wanted to be put on an ice floe and pushed offshore. The problem was, I lived above him on the iceberg and would be tasked with shoving him off.

In his bedroom, I stood over him, hesitating, phone in hand. His snores filled the room and there was a familiar scent of turmeric, garlic, and old man b.o. The heavy drapes were drawn. I had dreamt of his swift, painless passing—of coming downstairs one morning to find him gone, at peace at last. But I could not enter those dark waters. If I did, I didn't see how I'd ever come to ground again. So I dialed.

They arrived within minutes, sirens blaring. Ice floe hauled unceremoniously back to shore, into an ambulance, straight to the hospital on the hill.

Those first few days in the hospital, because my father was on a 72-hour psychiatric hold, an attendant sat in the room with him at all times. It was required, part of the procedure for attempted suicides, and purely bureaucratic and precautionary—he couldn't have hurt himself because he was unconscious. It turned out that the pills he had taken were Benadryl, repackaged and sold as an over-the-counter sleeping aid. He had downed the whole bottle, a hundred pills, but it wouldn't have killed him as he'd hoped. Nevertheless, he was unconscious for days, and when he finally woke he spoke in word salad. When speech eventually returned, he told me he'd had vivid waking dreams: Western epics scrolling in front of his eyes, wagon trains rolling through the room, and, once, me there in the scene, wrestling with a pack of unruly dogs.

I liked his mandated attendant and everyone else in that hospital, desperately. Most especially I liked Dr. A, the resident in charge of his care. Dr. A looked like a grown-up Harry Potter—dark hair, round black glasses, sweet pale face. He was born and raised in a country near the Adriatic that has seen much violence and suffering, and maybe because of this he had gravitas. Though he looked impossibly young he seemed like an old soul. At any rate, he was that rare thing, a serious person with a great sense of humor. He got a kick out of my father, who, once he could speak again, chatted him up on his daily rounds. Dad liked him, too.

Dad spoke at length about his decision to end his life with Dr. A, with Linda the Palliative Care Nurse Practitioner, with the young trio of psychiatrists who eventually decided he could be taken off psych hold. He was happy to share his end of life philosophy with them and saw no problem in what he'd done—though he acknowledged, when prodded, that it might have caused alarm. My father was indignant that the system could hold his life hostage to an ethic he did not accept, an infringement of what he saw as inalienable rights. In medical matters only, he was a staunch libertarian: *Keep your government hands off my death.*

My father pitched his case to Dr. A, and to the psych team. Dad asserted that he wasn't depressed. I wondered. His world had shrunk in recent years. His hearing aid had broken and he hadn't told me, afraid of the expense and bother of a replacement, and his vision, exacerbated by glaucoma, was steadily worsening. He felt less confident walking around the neighborhood and beyond our weekly shopping trip together and his visits to the doctor, he didn't get out much. He watched hours and hours of depressing news and bloviating pundits on MSNBC. To the medical team, he spoke about his right to choice, his lifelong interest in gerontology, and his spiritual convictions—he did not see death as a frightening end, merely a transmogrification of universal consciousness. He welcomed it: he wanted to be part of The Big Wow.

Nevertheless, the medical establishment replied, let's see if we can improve your situation here first. A plan for recovery was set, and he gamely considered all suggestions. He refused antidepressants but was open to seeing a therapist, and the psych team referred him to a psychiatric intern. I arranged to have his hearing aid fixed and switched his primary care physician to Dr. Z, who was recommended by Linda the Palliative Care Nurse.

Throughout, he charmed the staff and responded to the hospital routine with good-natured delight, as if he had stumbled, unplanned, into a five-star hotel. Often, I arrived at his room to find him holding court—with nurses, nursing aides, Dr. A, the social worker. He took the attention as his due and clearly felt it was his duty in turn to appreciate and entertain the people who were caring for him. In short, my father—who had railed against the medical establishment, who was born on a kitchen table in the Bronx in 1928 and had never once in eighty-nine years had a single hospital stay—was a model hospital patient.

It was a head-clearing, fifteen-minute walk from our house to the hospital. Each day for one long week I walked there and back, there and back. Professionals spoke to me privately in reassuring tones, offering referrals. Somebody gave me the number of an elder care specialist who could advise me on care options if I wanted. I wanted. I stood alone in a supply room at the end of the hall and had a long phone conversation with Ned the Elder Care Specialist. I told Ned the long saga of my father's case, how hard it had been. Surrounded by gallon jugs of cleaning fluid and boxes of non-latex gloves, I used Ned as one might use a therapist. I vented. Dad wouldn't admit when he needed help, he refused basic care and kept things from me, and everything related to his medical decisions was a struggle. Nothing I told Ned shocked him; he'd heard it all a thousand times before. "Sometimes you have to let them fail," he advised.

I spoke a few times to my father about the pain of his suicide attempt—his pain, and mine. I know I did, but I can't remember what I said other than, *please don't do that again.* Our interactions were often interrupted by the stream of specialists, a temporary safety net of services and assessments that I sank into with relief. We were carried along by the system and I was happy to have other voices in the mix that he would hopefully find more persuasive than mine. But I do remember this. A day or so before he was discharged, I asked, "Dad, did you consider how I might feel if you'd succeeded and had died right after we'd had that fight?"

In the months before he'd landed in hospital, my father's upper bridge had fallen out, soon followed by a lower bridge, and he was effectively toothless. He asserted that he wasn't in pain, could eat normally, and didn't care what he looked like. The UCSF School of Dentistry offers care at a sliding scale; he'd been a few times for fillings and checkups, and I pressured him to return for dentures. Over weeks of assessments, we'd learned that he was in for a lengthy process and an uncomfortable adjustment. In spite of my efforts at persuasion, he grew increasingly reluctant to go through with the plan.

I may be the villain of this story. I'm certainly not the hero. I know what I should have done for my father: let him make the decision to be toothless, as confounding as it was. He could still eat—he'd always talked with his mouth full and now, with no teeth but still plenty to say, he spat flecks of food all around his plate. Who did that hurt? I should have let it go, but I did not. We pushed each other into opposite corners.

Two days before the first step in the care plan that would finally bring him dentures, UCSF called him to confirm the appointment. He cancelled. When he told me the next day, anger hit physically, rising up through the soles of my feet. It would take weeks, even months to reschedule. I was about to start a new job and my future as shuttle service and caretaker to an obstinate old man stretched out to the horizon. I protested. He was unmoved.

In a voice shaking with anger, I said I was losing patience. Not only about the teeth. Losing patience with *him*. With every last thing about him.

"You look like a hobo, Dad."

He went downstairs and we didn't speak for the rest of the day. That night he took a bottle of sleeping pills and tried to die.

In the hospital, his face crumpled with remorse when I asked if he'd considered my feelings. He covered his eyes with his hand. "I'm sorry," he said, "I never meant."

It had honestly not occurred to him to consider my reaction. That moment of grief was the purest, truest emotion he showed, at least to me, about what he'd done, and it was fleeting. I don't think he could hold it for long. I don't blame him. It was heavy to hold.

My father cared deeply about vulnerable people—poor people, immigrants, the homeless, the forgotten and downtrodden. He had been a Catholic priest for ten years and took the vows hoping to work as a missionary in China. Though he didn't get the overseas job he'd wanted, he met my mother when they worked together at a Catholic university in upstate New York—so the priesthood changed the trajectory of his life, and hers, and is entirely responsible for mine.

While no longer Catholic, he was deeply spiritual, the more progressive the better. He adored *A Course in Miracles*—a kind of new age bible written (or "transcribed") in the mid-1960s by a psychologist named Helen Schucman who believed she was taking dictation directly from Jesus. I never read the book but he quoted it often, entranced by the concept of a modern Christianity fueled by love rather than atonement, without the painful dogma of original sin. (He would have thrilled to see the movement's famous evangelist, Marianne Williamson, emerge briefly on the national stage in 2019 as a Democratic presidential candidate. His dream ticket: Sanders/Williamson). My father circled again and again to a concept that was revolutionary to a recovering Catholic: we are all connected to God, everyone and everything, no separation. A battered, well-thumbed copy of the book stuffed with notes sat by his chair, in a place where in his early life he might have kept a Bible. Though I can't always muster it, I *want* to believe, like him, in a larger, kinder, more connected intelligence. His adamant faith filtered down to me as wistfulness leavened by skepticism, longing interspersed by flashes of spiritual insight and connection—a hunch rather than conviction.

He cared about the vulnerable but would not, *could not* admit that he was vulnerable himself. He had no assets—no house, no car, no savings—and a tiny fixed income; in San Francisco he qualified as "extremely low-income." He was eligible for Medi-Cal and other subsidies: less a safety net than a narrow, confusing set of hoops to jump through. He'd moved to California at my urging at age 80, after his previous arrangement, subletting a room from his older sister, ended when her health failed and her children moved her into a nursing home. He had nowhere else to go, and no backup plan. When he came west, it felt as though he leapt across the continent and I caught him.

And though my father could not abide being a burden, I often *did* feel burdened. His attempts to exert independence felt specifically designed to make my life harder. Nowhere was this battle more clearly drawn than over medical care.

For more than half of my childhood, until I was on my own after college and working in jobs that offered it, I was uninsured. As had been my mother, who had real need of it. She died just before age 60 after a series of strokes—she'd had high blood pressure for years but wasn't on medication, in part because her job didn't offer health insurance. Even after this catastrophe, my father was unshaken in his doctrine: Western medicine is not to be trusted. It was one of his central tenets beginning when I was ten years old—which happens to coincide with the time that he lost his job and we fell out of the middle class.

When I was a child, the guardrails holding our family on track were Vitamin C and pride. Why did our life become so chaotic and hard scrabble? My father had a hard time following rules. He had little impulse control and no filter, saying whatever flitted through his head, and he inevitably clashed with bosses and authority figures. He was tall, white, handsome, outgoing—he *looked* the part: the perfect patriarch. That opened doors, but the illusion quickly faded and he was fired from almost every job he ever held. Those jobs included: an administrator at a retirement home (twice, fired both times), an intergenerational community "thought leader," a 7-11 night shift worker, a toll taker at the airport, a nonprofit founder (with a tiny budget, no employees and a remote boss; this was his most lasting gig). He did not do well with rule-bound administrative tasks or bureaucracy, and I can't imagine he was a good employee—he was relentlessly optimistic but unpredictable in his reactions, prone to impractical ideas and bouts of frustrated anger that must have tried his coworkers' nerves. He was an enthusiast with unbounded, often unfounded confidence: a gold panner, the perfect mark for a flim-flam man. Once, a huckster roped him into a pyramid scheme selling some dubious product (vitamins? time shares? knife sets? I've blocked it out) to souls more trusting and hopeful than he. He couldn't find any.

For decades, his medical advice came from a 1970s-era vitamin book, tattered and stuffed with notes, another kind of bible. In the vitamin aisle, he'd never stint. Though he spent thousands on supplements and organic produce over the years, it was still far cheaper than medical care. For a time, it worked. I have no memory of either of my parents getting a checkup. I got sick, as kids do, and they took me to a strip mall emergency care clinic to treat ear infections or strep throat. I didn't suffer, they did not delay. I remember feeling awkward there, with strangers I'd never met and would likely not see again poking into my ears and mouth. Most of all, I was acutely aware that the bill was more than we could afford. I saw that in the way my mother pulled the checkbook from her purse, gripping the vinyl cover tightly.

But it's important to say that in my earliest memories my mother and I happily orbited around him. When he came home from work, he must have paused, changed clothes, kissed my mother, had a few moments of transition—but in my memory, every day, as soon as he walked in the door I demanded his attention and got it. Up on the bed! I yelled, at ages two, three, four, and there we'd be, me bouncing and leaping on my parents' enormous king size mattress and my father catching me, raising me high, laughing as hard as I was. He was the sun our household revolved around, and the person I was happiest to see. And he seemed equally ecstatic to walk in the door and find me there, waiting for him.

My father was not one thing. And in the end, those same qualities that had caused so much upheaval allowed him to bluster his way to a chosen exit with nothing but force of will and confidence. That's not to say he didn't suffer. No one gets out unscathed.

Before he was discharged from his weeklong hospital stay, Dad had a few sessions with a physical therapist and it became clear that mobility was a pressing challenge. His wiry strength had severely dissipated and he now required a walker and plenty of patience. We received special instructions about how to handle stairs—I was to stand behind him, hand on the belt at the small of his back, as he carefully, slowly, maneuvered himself and the walker.

At home, we scurried to get his downstairs apartment ready: a more stable armchair for the living room (his favorite rocker was no longer steady enough) and grab bars for his bed. The post-hospitalization

Medicare system kicked in, and those first weeks were full of appointments: home visits from a physical therapist, a nurse's aide to help with bathing, a social worker. I drew up a family contract and printed it out in 16-point font and we each signed it—*ask for help when needed, stay open minded about suggested medical care, hugs when requested, no self-harm*. I drove him to therapy appointments, and to a place that retested him for a hearing aid, and to his new primary care physician, Dr. Z, a short gay man in his 60s with a dramatic red moustache and a reassuring manner.

On our first visit it became clear that Dr. Z, though kind and a good listener, was not inclined to humor my father's alternative medicine inclinations. He reviewed the long list of vitamins and supplements Dad took and said that for the most part, there was no scientific basis for taking them. My father looked puzzled. They were polite but on different wavelengths. "Great socks," Dad offered, looking for a point of connection. It was true. Dr. Z wore fantastic, colorful socks. To my mind, that was enough. Unlike Dad's previous doctor, an elderly physician who ran a stunningly inefficient, jam-packed office in the middle of congested Chinatown, Dr. Z's office was nearby and the wait blessedly short.

They were simpatico on one important point. Dad told Dr. Z how strongly he wanted his death to be self-directed and Dr. Z did not disagree. He told us he'd had experience with the End of Life Option Act, which went into effect in California in 2016, and had prescribed help for terminal patients who wanted a peaceful end. But my father did not fit the guidelines. Outside of being eighty-nine and having a heart condition, glaucoma, macular degeneration, edema, deafness, arrhythmia, high blood pressure … aside from those things he was doing all right. He was old, yes, but none of his conditions was terminal. Dr. Z could not step outside the bounds of the law, though he understood my father's desire not to lose independence. "Some people just stop eating when they're ready to go," he told Dad casually. "If you stop taking fluids, too, stop drinking, then things can happen quickly, in a matter of a few days."

My father perked up at this. He got quiet for a moment and looked almost cheerful. He filed it away, I think, until Christmas.

I was so relieved that Dr. Z took Dad on as a patient I wanted to hug him, or cry. But I didn't. I rarely cried during those months. At least, I can't remember doing so. I felt as if I had superpowers of energy and focus. I made sure he took his pills each day and arranged appointments and drove him to them and ordered things online and cooked and called in Meals on Wheels. I fulfilled the duties of my new job and went to meetings and did laundry and walked the dogs and went grocery shopping. I soldiered through, a workaday beetle in a hard carapace.

Some weeks later I had dinner with a writer friend and told her the saga of Dad's attempted suicide, how he'd swallowed a bottle of sleeping pills that turned out to be mostly Benadryl. She'd had her own struggles: a troubled daughter, including some hospitalizations. "Benadryl?" she said, with the wry tone of someone who's been in the trenches. "He didn't do his homework."

He didn't do his homework. That could be the tagline for so many of his choices. Did I wish he'd done his homework? Sometimes, yes, I did.

The post-hospitalization Medicare-funded visits ended, and we were on our own again. I looked into

Medi-Cal support for nursing aides; the co-pay was shockingly high for a benefit purportedly for poor people, but it didn't matter—Dad refused ongoing help, claimed he didn't need it, even though the thought of him maneuvering his unsteady body in and out of the shower on his own filled me with anxiety. After a few weeks of compliance to our contract, he began to reassert his independence. I would have taken this as a good sign if he weren't still so frail, but his impaired mobility was worrisome. He did the physical therapy exercises faithfully but never regained his prior strength—he needed the walker for weeks, and then a cane, and was troubled by edema in his legs. He was never able to come with me to the co-op grocery store again, an outing he'd always loved, and he struggled to walk up the stairs to our apartment for Thanksgiving dinner. He struggled generally, and it wasn't just his mobility. He was depressed. All the expert help did not change the hard fact of his increasing frailty.

Over Thanksgiving weekend, we had to make a trip to an emergency clinic and then to the ER to treat Dad's edema, which had turned his legs into cracked swollen sausages. The following Monday, we went to see Dr. Z.

Dad was tired, walking with difficulty. His weeping legs left wet stains on his sweatpants. Dr. Z prescribed a diuretic and compression socks that were hard to manage—he couldn't wrangle them himself, and I helped him peel them on and off each morning and night.

I was trying desperately to keep it together in my new job. My wife helped as she could, but she was traveling across the country frequently, caring for her own sick parent, a mother with advanced cancer. I was wound tight, sharper and hardier than I'd had any inkling I could be. We come up against ourselves in middle age, reckoning with the gap between what we'd imagined for ourselves and what we actually are—a whistling chasm that I stepped over so quickly I scarcely had time to mourn. There was too much to do. For a time, all I could eat was Triscuits and cream cheese. And white wine, more than was good for me. I leaned on the colorless comfort as we entered the penultimate phase of my father's life, an experience that still fills me with a nameless feeling, a spectrum with polarities related to but more complicated than gratitude and dread.

On Christmas morning, we rose early, drank coffee. My wife made a special breakfast, Eggs in Purgatory, a savory, baked egg and tomato treat we knew Dad would love. I went downstairs to get him so he could come up for breakfast and gifts, as was our tradition. He wore the sweatpants I'd bought him—loose, with the elastic bands cut so they wouldn't bind his ankles. I put heavy lotion on his legs and helped him on with the compression socks. He grabbed his walker. "We'll take it slow," I said. One step over and out the sliding glass back door and then an incline upward, over rough old cement, and past the laundry room. Then three steps to get to the backyard. After that, six more steps up to our back door. I took his left side, held the small of his back as he prepared to take the three steps into the yard. Dad held the railing with his right hand and stood, psyching himself up. He took one step with difficulty and stopped. "Better not," he said.

"You want to turn around?" I could scarcely believe it. I'd never seen him admit to physical weakness.

"Better not," he confirmed, defeated. I helped him back into his apartment, to the chair in front of the television. We brought breakfast down and opened presents next to the small Christmas tree I'd set up on the little table near his armchair.

He loved Eggs in Purgatory, eating with relish. But he was uncharacteristically quiet after breakfast, deflated. That afternoon, when I went downstairs to check in, he told me his plan. "I'm ready. I'm going to stop eating."

Here is where memory, among other things, fails me. At some point in those weeks, when he was worrying over loss of independence and the slow pace of his recovery, I reminded him of what Dr. Z had said. "You won't wind up hospitalized and stuck forever. You can always stop eating, no one can force you to do anything." Did he think I was giving him a nudge, conveying a wish that he be gone? I never imagined he'd do it. He loved food, *all* food, and ate everything, from elaborate epicurean meals to peanut butter sandwiches, with delight. The fridge in his kitchen was full of meals and snacks I couldn't imagine him leaving untouched—the waste alone would pain him.

Trying to reconstruct these events, I become shaky, second-guessing. I want to remember this in a way that clarifies whether or not I'm culpable. I remember feeling cautious, trying to be diplomatic and not alarmist. I do know, I'm certain that I said to him: "Dad, I don't want to tell you what to do, but you can change your mind at any point. There's no shame at all in that." The next day, he drank some juice but did not eat. He was proud when he told us this, surprisingly peppy—he seemed full of a familiar purpose, even hope, in a way that he hadn't been since his hospitalization. Several days passed and I kept expecting to find him sitting downstairs with a favorite snack, a plate of Ak-Mak crackers slathered in almond butter and apricot jam, or toast with scrambled eggs. But I never saw him eat again after Eggs in Purgatory. I kept waiting for his exit strategy to be another failed experiment, an abandoned attempt. He kept going.

I could not write during this time. Luckily, he did. He decided to "document his journey" and wrote voluminously on a legal pad. Reading through his post-Christmas notes, I'm reminded that I took him to consult with Dr. Z on the 28th. It settles me a little bit, seeing this confirmation. My therapist once posited that my father had a false self—he had little grounding and therefore presented a constructed persona to the world, and to me. It struck me as true. I said more than once that *he* was only person convinced by his schemes and dreams—but that's not entirely true. He created smoke and mirrors for me, too. It was difficult to hold onto specifics after fraught interactions—he left me confused, befuddled. My compartmentalized brain could handle what was thrown at it with some adeptness in the moment but couldn't hold onto much.

Did it really happen the way I remember? Can what he did be one of the bravest things a person can do and also an act of ego and delusion?

"Christmas Day, Monday (12/25/17). A lovely visit with Genanne and Lauren while I enjoyed the special breakfast they had prepared and brought down to my apartment. I decided not to attempt the trip up the back stairs for their traditional breakfast and gift opening. During the leisurely chat while eating I experienced the distinct sense of arriving—not striving—for the oneness that, at this point in my journey, is a green light that I can depart (the body) and be on my way to whatever the Light

experience is." Below this, he transcribed a quote from *A Course in Miracles* related to universal oneness.

"*Wednesday, December 27, '17. Genanne and Lauren sat for a long visit and I mentioned to them that I was ready to let go and say goodbye. Typically they were perfectly accepting though saddened (What a great duo!). Genanne's comment summed up her/their choice and action throughout: "I'm here for you Dad." (So I mulled over an unusual New Year's event.)*"

He really thought that not eating between Christmas and New Year's would do the trick. He believed he would die in a matter of days. Later in his notes, he recorded that his last meal was toast and tea on Wednesday, the 27th.

At Dr. Z's office the next day, Dad told the doctor what he was doing. He was convinced and convincing: this was his right and he was ready. Dr. Z listened intently. They spoke for more than an hour. Dr. Z assessed my father's soundness and agreed. He put a referral to hospice and a prescription for morphine into the computer system, and advised that we call the hospice service straight away. It would be covered by Medicare. On the way out the door, he told me to call him anytime.

Dad left in a great mood. My skinny father with the weeping legs and gleaming eyes—he'd got what he'd wanted, Dr. Z had taken him seriously. Suddenly there was a realness to what was happening. Maybe this wasn't just another of his half-baked schemes. I clung to the phone number for hospice and felt overwhelming love for the office building with its adjacent parking garage, and for the convenient little pharmacy window on the first floor, where I dropped off the prescription for morphine. Dad waited in the lobby while I went to get the car, sitting ramrod straight and beaming at everyone who walked by. In the parking garage, I felt affection even for the irritating auto-pay machine, which spat out my dollars like a finicky child. There was a path forward. Others had walked it, there were guideposts, and the medical system would actually help us. A refrain churned through my head: *Not alone, not alone, not alone.*

That afternoon, we moved his bed into his living room so he could stretch out in the room he used most, watch TV, and enjoy more natural light. We set up a bedside table: water and a sponge to moisten his lips (Dr. Z had recommended this, reminding Dad that drinking juice or water would prolong things). He had his writing pad and pens nearby, and books he wanted. Lauren and I spent time downstairs, talking and watching basketball games. I wrote Dad a letter of gratitude, thanking him for what he'd given me, and printed it out for him in large font.

Recalling this makes me feel disembodied. Did I really do those things?

"Hospice will help you," Dr. Z had promised. "Nurses will check in on you daily. You'll be comfortable." I looked up the place as soon as we got home. Even the website was spa-like, soothing.

What was I hoping for? For it to be everything he wanted: self-directed, swift. We would have opportunities for resolution and forgiveness and goodbyes. In that, we were on the same page. I also wanted release, peace, simplicity—not for him, for myself. I wanted to be done playing dutiful daughter and nagging harpy. I wanted freedom from resentment that I was doing so much for him and shame that I wasn't doing enough. So it's accurate to say that at the end of his life, I was his accomplice. I scarcely argued against his decision. I believed, truly, that he wanted to go. It would also release me. Do my feelings matter, if it was what he wanted? Do you hear my guilt in that question?

"Friday, Dec 29. Slept til eight a.m.! "Bird bath" and then these notes. Expect visit from Hospice this afternoon."

A young man named Jonathan knocked on the door, right on time. He wore khakis and a blue shirt and spoke softly, a reassuring presence right from the start. We'd been waiting nervously, as if it were a first date. We three sat together in Dad's living room. Afternoon light poured in over his bed by the window. Jonathan leaned forward, listening, and made it clear he understood and respected my father's wishes. I had the distinct feeling that he brought not just help, but succor in the spiritual sense. There was something otherworldly about his gentleness. Jonathan was like a young priest—not the contemporary, suspect variety, but a true believer from the old days, vibrating on a higher frequency. We could see that hospice was his calling, not merely his job—he wanted to help people at the intersection of life and death, to facilitate those moments when we can grasp the power and the mystery. He spoke fluently with my father when Dad shared his philosophical and spiritual feelings about death, and told us about the ways hospice would help, what we could expect. Jonathan would not be the one on call but the nurses were first rate, and we could call the hospice for help at any time. He handed me a resource binder, mine to keep.

It was nothing less than a love connection. Dad beamed, vibrating on Jonathan's frequency. I felt it, too. Oh, Jonathan, with your kind face and binder full of helpful color-coded tabs. My jaw and shoulders unclenched for the first time in months.

The winter sun was fading when Jonathan said it was time for him to call the office and get a sign off from the attending physician. My father's files had been transferred the day before, and presumably the hospice powers-that-be had reviewed his chart. This visit was only procedural. I switched on the lights and Jonathan went to stand in the kitchen to make the call. Dad and I looked at each other, his expression approving. I relaxed into the cushion underneath me. After a few minutes on the phone, Jonathan's tone shifted. Something was not right. The supervising physician had to make another call, Jonathan told us, and would call him right back. A tendril of dread pushed up, shadows stretching across the wall. When the doctor called back, Jonathan walked further from us into the hall. His gentle voice had changed, flattened. "What should I tell them?" I heard. "How can I—"

I looked at the tidy binder of resources in my lap. My father—either because he was hard of hearing or convinced of his rights—was slower on the uptake. But he must have suspected that the length of time was odd. Eventually, Jonathan came back into the room and said in a hushed voice, "I am so sorry. There's a problem. The attending physician needs to talk to you." He handed the phone to me, his face grave. I took it and walked into the kitchen.

The doctor's voice was taut. She introduced herself and told me she'd gone over my father's file more thoroughly and had consulted with another physician. Because Dad did not have a presenting terminal condition they could not move forward.

"But Dr. Z told us you would help," I said, already hopeless.

"Well, he had the wrong information. I can't explain it. Sometimes older doctors don't keep up with all the new...." She could not legally sign off on this plan. "I am so sorry," she said. "I'd like to be able to help you, but I can't. I wish the laws were different."

"Me too." My stomach hurt. I badly wanted to get off the phone and lie down.

"There's something else." She spoke slowly, trying to land the news gently, as you might tell someone they have a terminal condition. "Because your father is not eating and has tried before to end his life, I am legally required to report him for a wellness check."

Report him?

"To the police. For a wellness check. I have to do it because—"

"Because you're a mandated reporter." I used the term to let her know I wasn't an idiot, and she could stop speaking so slowly.

"Listen," she said. "I have to call them, but you don't have to answer the door. You don't have to speak to them. Or if you do speak to them you can be prudent about the answers. I'm going to have them ask him two questions and all he has to say is no and they'll leave him alone. I'm just going to tell them to ask, 'Are you a danger to yourself? Are you a danger to others?' That's it." She tried to make it sound easy: police at the door, no worries. "I am so sorry," she repeated. "I wish I didn't have to but I could—"

"Lose your license. All right."

I handed the phone to Jonathan. He spoke to her again, his voice curt. Jonathan was angry. I wouldn't have guessed he had it in him. After he hung up he apologized to us profusely, clearly miserable, and hovered, lingering longer than he should have. He explained to my father why everything he'd been promised was being taken away. "The laws just aren't there yet," Jonathan said. He was paler than when he'd arrived.

She had called the cops by now, they were surely en route. *Do not say you're sorry one more time, Jonathan.* I showed him to the door, where he stood on the stoop, reluctant to leave. "You need to make sure this doesn't happen again, because it feels terrible." He looked stricken, apologized one last time, and I shut the door in his face.

I turned to my father. "Did you hear everything?" I asked. He hadn't, not quite. "The police are going to come," I explained. "If you tell them you're not eating and drinking they'll take you to the hospital." He protested. "It's the law, Dad, the law doesn't care about what you want. If you don't want them to take you in, you're going to have to lie." I had to make sure he understood this very clearly. It may seem strange that I had to spell it out—but he'd always had a guilelessness, an innocent belief in the rightness of his convictions, and he'd never seen the point of dissembling. Also, he'd never paid much attention to norms and rules. He was truly baffled that anyone might tell him he couldn't die as he wanted. We had a few minutes, but only a few. I explained as best as I could, relaying what the doctor had said.

When the state knocks at your door, sometimes it is a social worker in sensible shoes, but more often it's these guys. The knock was as loud and assertive as Jonathan's had been gentle. Two police cars were pulled haphazardly in front of the house, lights flashing, and three uniformed officers filed into the room, burly and full of adrenaline. They each had close-cropped hair, muscled arms, guns on their hips, and one-syllable names: Juan. Dan, Will. Not one looked to be over twenty-five.

"How you *doing*?" Will, the one in charge, boomed at Dad, eyes scanning the room.

My father boomed back, "Couldn't be better!"

Will asked my Dad the hospice doctor's questions. He answered firmly, in his biggest, roundest voice. No, he was not a danger to himself or others. No and no.

He certainly didn't look it. Dad sat in the chair in his cardigan, legs up on the ottoman and a book in his lap. The room smelled of Sleepytime tea. As Will questioned Dad, the other two cops walked through the apartment, down the hall to the bedroom, checking for weapons or hostages or body bags. They filed back into the living room and nodded at Will, giving the all clear. Everything about them leaned toward action, and the energy in the room was hyped, a strong current of testosterone. Dad chatted about the Warriors game scheduled for that night.

"How about we take you into the hospital and you can get checked out?"

"No need! I'm great here."

"We were just going to have a quiet evening and watch the game," I added.

The lights from their cars shone through the windows and flashed red on the walls. I wondered, in some compartment of my lizard brain, why it was necessary to send two cars and three officers to perform a wellness check on one old man.

A radio crackled and the third cop left abruptly, called to another crisis. Will wasn't ready to let it go. "How about we take him in," he repeated, to me this time.

"*Please.* He's eighty-nine and just wants to watch basketball in peace."

This argument seemed to hold some weight. Does a danger to self or others care about the Warriors? Full darkness had fallen, though it was just shy of six o'clock. Will had the authority to do whatever he wanted and we all knew it. For a moment, it seemed inevitable that no matter what he said Dad would be swept back to the hospital with his wrists strapped down. I did my best to project calm and match my father's friendly, casual tone. Nothing to see here, officer.

Dad kept chattering, moving on to his second favorite sports subject, the Giants. His gift of gab sealed the deal somehow—or maybe another call on the radio promised better action elsewhere. They left.

All of it, from Jonathan to the blue wave, had taken place over the course of two hours. I felt like I'd been punched in the gut then backed over by a midsize SUV. Upstairs, fingers shaking, I dialed Dr. Z's pager. He called right away.

Dr. Z must have had a conversation with the hospice doc, because he didn't sound surprised when I relayed what had happened. "There was a misunderstanding," he said, haltingly. Passive voice: mistakes were made. I told him it had been very difficult. "Oh, I'm so sorry." He sounded old himself, and genuinely apologetic.

"Dad wants to stay home," I said. "He's committed, and I want to help him, but we can't go through something like that again."

"No," he said. "You shouldn't have to." He paused. "You have to be careful, you know." He told me that if Dad died at home alone without hospice care it would trigger an automatic inquest, and I could potentially, worst case scenario, be accused of elder abuse. "It would be best not to let that happen. You can help him but you have to be very careful."

He talked me through options, all of them fraught. I could wait until he fails and call 911 when he became unconscious, close to the end but still alive.

"I don't think I can do that," I said.

"Ah," he said, "yes." It was so close to New Year's. I wondered what colorful socks Dr. Z was wearing that night. "Call me at any point," he said.

I did not sleep that night, imagining the questions I'd be asked if an emaciated old man died under my care—not nearly so easy as the questions the cops had asked us that night. Am I a danger to myself or others?

My father kept up his notes. He was writing, at this point, with an eye toward a future audience.

"*Friday 12/29/17. PM visit from hospice worker. He was very helpful and after consultation confirmed that they could not be helpful in my personal choice to abstain (for now) from food or water. Later (around 6?) a visit from several SFPD officers to "check-in." Found no assistance needed and left shortly. Nice guys! (And sharp/informed!). Watched Warriors get walked over by Utah. Genanne went to bed by halftime. Lauren stayed until almost the bitter end. Lights out by twelve and slept til eight (!). With two wake-ups when I knocked something off the night table. (Even asleep, the body "habit" follows the old format). Hmmm—a future essay on that physical lesson applied to the larger, metaphysical reality…"*

For the next day or two, we kept on much the same. We offered him food and he waved it off, saying he felt fine and was surprised at how comfortable he was. He kept to his routine. Shaving in the morning ("splashing his face"), dressing. His only concession to a new way of being (or dying) were the sweatpants and slippers. Before, he'd always dressed for the day in pants and shoes.

I went to check on him as soon as I woke. That morning he was in the bathroom, a towel wrapped around his waist and another slung over his shoulders. His new cane hung on the bathroom sink. I'd taken a load of clothes out of the dryer and handed him clean sweatpants and a t-shirt. He patted his face dry, pulled the towel off his shoulders and dropped it to the floor, waving his hand. "Thanks, Hon. There's another mess for you to clean up."

Often when my father spoke his words fell into some obscure landfill in my brain, not clearly computed. Lauren was helpful in that regard, serving as a reality check for conversations when he suddenly said something so off base or clueless that I'd never have remembered on my own. But those particular words entered my body and stuck. I remember the blue morning light in the bathroom exactly, the clean scent of his shaving cream, steam on the mirror, and where we both stood. Another mess for me to clean up.

Nothing much changed that day. The swelling was down in his legs. Lauren and I speculated about whether he was eating, but if he did we never saw it. He had no dip in energy, no confusion or light-headedness. He seemed more vibrant, clarified, a hunger artist honed to his essential self. He was lit by some inner fire, his eyes gleamed, his face almost incandescent. In short, he loved having our attention and was having a pretty good time.

That night the three of us sat downstairs, talking. Which is to say, my wife and I listened while he held court. He reminisced about my mother, which led him to remember her final illness. When she was fifty-nine, she'd had a stroke that landed her in the hospital and months of rehab, and then, about six months later, a much larger stroke that was the beginning of the end. That night, he told a story I'd never heard. When he'd called the ambulance after her second stroke, "The EMT reamed me a new one."

"Why?" I asked, confused. Because, he told us, he'd waited to call 911. For over an hour, he had "monitored her," and not dialed for help. He'd told the EMTs this when they asked how long she had been nonresponsive, as scrupulously honest about his inexplicable choices as he'd always been. He did not explain his thinking to us. Maybe he thought she'd snap out of it. More likely, he wanted to see if she'd die a natural death, unimpeded. Maybe, too, he was exhausted and ready to be done with caregiving. Then it went on too long and he got scared and called the ambulance. It was a story he'd never told me, not once in the two decades since her death, and that in itself was clarifying. He was ashamed of it—he'd lost her precious time and he knew how it would land. All the things he'd touted most vociferously as elements of a "good death"—at home, under hospice care, avoiding hospitals and nursing homes like the plague—were not things granted to my mother. After her first series of strokes, she spent time in hospital and rehabilitated in a nursing home—and she'd died in a hospital, given morphine generously or stingily depending upon the nurse on shift.

Upstairs, when I asked my wife what she remembered about that conversation she said that she couldn't look at my face when he'd told us. He had done exactly what you *shouldn't* do with a stroke victim. The negligence stunned me. Had he been cruel, or clueless? How could I know for sure? I told Lauren, "I have to get him out of here. I can't do it anymore." I have no memory of anything else that night.

"*Dec. 31, 2017. Slept til 6 a.m. with two major nighttime pees (1 pint???). Still have not swallowed or chewed anything since Wednesday morning. No hunger pangs yet, or cravings. I recall during the night (2a.m.?) waking to a fairly rapid throb on my left side. I was sleeping on my left hip and heard the throb in my left palm, which was under my face. Huh? Is this the day my ticker finally says goodbye? I (sort of) hope so. Genanne and Lauren continue to offer options, food, etc. They are amazingly supportive while honoring my choice. Gracias! Peace!"*

The next morning, New Year's Day, I told him I would take him to the hospital. It was too much, I explained, there was too much that could go wrong. And here's the thing: he came willingly. He did not put up an argument, almost leaping into the car, more agile than he'd been in months. Did he know, some part of him, how I'd react to that story about Mom? Did he want to shift things, push toward another kind of conclusion? Perhaps. But it's entirely possible, even likely, that he had no plan whatsoever. That, too, was my father. A mystifying combination—genially accommodating, monstrously self-involved, and always confounding.

After the ER doc talked to Dad and reviewed his file, it was clear we were going down a familiar path. Another 72-hour hold. They'd keep him in the ER until they could transfer him to the geriatric psych ward across town, a move that would likely happen later that night. This doc reminded me a bit of the cops—macho, certain. He listened to my father talk about his decision but didn't really hear him. Outside the room, he asked me, if any sort of medical crisis should happen while Dad was there, not that he expected one, did I want to authorize medical intervention? I was floored. He'd just spent fifteen minutes talking to my father about his end of life wishes. "All the documentation is in his file," I snapped. "He's said very clearly that the last thing he wants is intervention." The EMT standing at the desk looked up at me, and then back down.

I drove home, collapsing on the couch for an hour or two. When I returned to the hospital Dad wasn't in the ER. Everything had changed. Dr. A was on duty that night, had seen my father's name come over the transom, remembered him, and went down to check in.

If Dr. A had not been working that day. Or if he'd been exhausted and let my father's name slide past on the screen, moving on to the next record. If he'd been busy with other patients and not had time to go down to chat, had left Dad in the clutches of the ER doc and the geriatric psych ward. But Dr. A stepped in and diverted the plan.

Dr. A transferred my father upstairs, under his care. He arranged to have the psych team—the same residents who had seen Dad a few months prior—reassess him. He let my father refuse food and did not pressure him to eat, although the hospital catering department called the phone at his bedside three times a day to ask if he wanted a meal. Dad always refused. He continued to drink some water, had glossed over what Dr. Z had told him about not drinking fluids, holding onto only the advice that suited him. Dr. A scheduled an echocardiogram to diagnose my father's heart trouble more specifically. He searched for something and found it: a heart condition that could legally justify my father's chosen exit, if he really wanted it. After a few days of tests and assessments, he said my father could carry on. They would not strap his wrists or intubate or treat him as if he were crazy. They wouldn't stop him. When the trio of psychiatrists huddled with me at the door to Dad's room and told me they wouldn't put him on psych hold this time, I burst into tears. I told them, and Dr. A, that it was the most humane working of a medical system I'd likely ever witness.

My father took it as his due. Again, this second time in hospital, Dad was a model patient and the staff loved him. One nurse went out of her way to tell me reassuring things; she wanted me to know she thought I was doing the right thing for him. I had the sense that we were the ward favorites, which pleased me more than I liked to admit.

The two of us spent hours together, as much as when he'd been home but cocooned within the reassuring rhythms of a bustling hospital. So long as we had help, I felt I could handle anything. I brought him the newspaper and his favorite new age books and read them aloud. I felt closer to him than I had since early childhood, as devoted and eager to spend time together as when he'd arrive home from work to lift me high overhead. He remained perky and clear-headed, said he felt no discomfort and still believed he'd die any day—though he was as strong as a rangy dog. One morning, when he told Dr. A he expected to expire within the next 24 hours, the doc looked at him and laughed a little, warning it could very well be longer than that. This assessment from a medical expert did not faze my father.

Our favorite nurse, a lanky woman in her 50s, came by one afternoon to help him stand on his feet so he could visit the bathroom. "We should go dancing, you and me," she joked, "you're nice and tall."

"I used to be," Dad said, undeniable sadness in his voice. He did not dwell in that sadness, though he had hours (upon hours, upon days) to consider it. At this point, we were waiting for hospice. The hospital social worker had talked me through the options and recommended a hospice facility only a few blocks from home. We just had to wait for "a bed to open up."

One afternoon I came back from lunch and Dad had been moved to a large private room. His roommate, a young man coming off a bad trip, had caused some sort of disruption and they'd pulled Dad out of that cramped space and into a peaceful, light-filled room at the end of the hall.

"What a view!" Dad said. For a hospital room it was the Ritz, with big, westward facing windows. We gazed contentedly out over the trees. If he could have stayed there for the rest of his days we'd both have been perfectly happy.

As it was, the following Monday a hospice space was confirmed and the last EMTs of his life came to deliver us to his final stop: a yellow, two-story building across the street from Most Holy Redeemer Catholic Church, on a quiet street in the Castro. It had once been a convent and then, during the AIDS crisis, cared for young men stricken in their prime. Dad had a small room with a window, a sink, and pale blue walls, with a saccharine-pastel mural of a meadow on the wall near the bed. He didn't think much of the room, mostly because the tiny TV that hung over his bed did not have cable—he really missed MSNBC.

"Come on," I said, to distract him. "Let's take a tour." I wheeled him to the end of the hall, into a large, beautiful wood-paneled room with stained glass windows and comfortable chairs and bookshelves. The far side of the room had a dais with a chessboard and two overstuffed armchairs. An older man who looked perfectly healthy sat there reading a book. Dad was uncharacteristically quiet, almost sullen. He was coming to terms with the fact that this was his final stop. I would not bring him home. He didn't ask, but I'm sure he wondered. Why couldn't I give him the one thing he wanted, death in his own bed?

On his second or third day at hospice, Dad told me crossly that the room I loved so much, the library with the stained glass, was the room where the priest would have conducted service for the nuns, back in the days when the building was a convent. The dais was in fact a pulpit where the priest stood to bless wine and bread, transubstantiated to the blood and the flesh. Then I understood how much he didn't like the place. He was unhappy with the reminders of his forsworn Catholicism—but mostly because he was there with strangers, unmistakably the end of the line, and he kept outliving his predictions. Every day, he asserted that the next day would be his last. But as time wore on reality came down in a way it hadn't in the bustling hospital. Unlike the hospital, hospice was *quiet*. Hospice was time, unadulterated.

I went to sit with him in the mornings, left for lunch, returned in the afternoons and then again after dinner. I tracked a path to hospice, a ten minute walk from our house, so frequently I imagined my feet left grooves in the sidewalk: 17th to Castro to 18th to Diamond. 17th to Market to Collingwood to 18th to Diamond. Sometimes, for a change of pace, Hartford to 19th to Diamond. And back again, and again, my world a taut network of veins that cut between two organs, his heart and mine, streets I'd known for decades but would never walk the same way again.

One afternoon I bumped into the hospice pastor, just finishing her rounds: a warm, middle-aged Black woman. She was smart, personable, and asked questions about my life that had nothing to do with being the daughter of a dying person. After we'd chatted awhile, she told me she had talked with Dad and noticed that, while he was very committed to his choice, he seemed to lack a humility that comes over the dying, a sign that a person has grappled with what's to come and arrived at a peaceful acceptance of transience. "He could go on for much longer than you think," she warned. Or at least, it felt like a warning. I wasn't entirely sure what to think when death-and-dying professionals spoke to me—I did not quite believe that they were really going to let him have his way. I half expected her to grab me by the shoulders and demand, *What's really going on here? What kind of terrible daughter are you?*

No one did this. But she, with her caution and searching gaze, came closest. "He's never been a humble person," I told her. "That's just his way of communicating."

"Nevertheless," she said. "I've seen people last months." She gave me her card, told me to call any time, and promised to check on him the following week.

We went on. Lauren and I brought our dogs to visit him once, and they panted on the floor, perhaps alarmed at the layered smells in that place. Our friend Alice met us in the neighborhood for dinner and came to visit, bringing Dad an orchid. Cards appeared from cousins, and I tacked them to the corkboard near his bed. I'd kept some of the closer cousins updated, but I hadn't told them that his visit to hospice was self-driven. I was afraid of judgment, that we'd be lectured, or shunned. (I think, now, that I just didn't give them the benefit of the doubt, a learned self-censorship: keep away from the shame-based secrets, best face forward.)

Any day now, he'd say each day…as if saying it would make it so. It was as if he was holding an argument with himself—the story he was telling butting up against the fact of the body. For a while it seemed that he gained energy with every day. He could, and did, talk for hours.

He wasn't strong enough to walk around but sat upright in his wheelchair, vibrating with energy. His eyes blazed, his mind was clear. And what his mind wanted was to be felt in the world, darting along channels that were dear to him: spirituality, politics, his family tree.

A range of hospice volunteers cycled through, including a group of a cappella singers who crowded into the room and sang "You Are My Sunshine." There was a doctor who made periodic rounds, though I never met him, and an administrator with an office on the first floor. Each visit, I rang the doorbell and signed in and the nurses in the front office greeted me—they had a locked cabinet full of drugs to help with pain, anxiety, hallucinations, and other ailments of the seriously ill. My father refused them all, saying he wasn't uncomfortable. As at the hospital, he could ask for food whenever he wanted, but he refrained. The nurse aides, all of them women immigrants, many Filipinas, were on call round-the-clock, and a buzzer attached to his bed that he could ring for help at any time. But for long stretches of his day, no professionals intervened. The work of death, in the end, is an individual labor. Each time I walked out the door, I could not escape the feeling that I was abandoning him there. And yet, I would have cut off my arm before bringing him home.

"*It is now Friday, January 12, 2018. About yesterday, I noticed that in the wheelchair visit with Genanne and Lauren, about 4p.m, I was describing new body signals. Shortness of breath. Lightheaded a bit and blurry vision. More noticeable "pulling" in heart area. Not painful and not forced. Later, in bed, I experienced a shift in my focus: letting go of the body issues to accepting the spirit/oneness. Now focus I always have.*"

At this point he hadn't eaten or taken his blood pressure medication for three weeks. He liked to sit in front of the sink in his room, shaving and splashing his face every morning. He was surely drinking water, and thus extending his life, though he never drank in front of me.

He'd dreamed of a swift, painless passing but came up hard against the reality of it—the fact of the body— hungry, pained, stiff, noisy, itchy, bored, thinking thinking thinking. Letting go of *that* is another thing entirely. Time wore on and he grew thinner but maintained an almost frantic energy. Each day he seemed more vital. He kept outpacing all of his confident predictions, the "this'll be the day" bluster. He did not look or act like a man who hadn't eaten in weeks. I had moments, sitting at his bedside, when panic rose and it felt like he'd never let go, never release me from being his audience.

He doesn't have the requisite humility, the pastor had warned; she'd put the fear into me, fear of being caught in an endless loop with this man who expected so much. At night, I'd lie in bed replaying our interactions and had an eerie feeling that so long as I showed up to listen, he'd keep talking, growing stronger and reedier and more demanding. I still feel a rush of primal adrenaline at the memory, a sense of desperate self-preservation. Some nights I lay in bed wishing fervently for release, for both of us: a prayer and a curse jumbled together. *Please just let go, just fucking die. Please die.*

The lack of cable news continued to dismay him. He had used MSNBC like addicts use a fix—a hit of adrenaline, diversion from personal pain that would not or could not be addressed. Instead, I read him the newspaper and poems he loved. Sometimes he had flashes of a more contemplative kind of reflection, a searching that reached inward rather than pushing outward. "I took you and your mother for granted," he said once. But it was not his natural state, and it did not last long. He wanted death so badly but at the same time was eager to keep searching, to know things, to carve an imprint in words that would be indelible. But isn't that what we all want? I am here, I matter.

One afternoon he was in a foul, impatient mood. Lauren and I were both there, and he had asked me to cut his nails but kept fidgeting as I tried to wield the clippers. Then he said offhandedly that we were being sneaky, scheming or conspiring against him. We asked what he meant and he backtracked immediately, said his mind was foggy. But it felt perilous. Suddenly the rules had changed.

Walking home, stunned, I asked Lauren, "What just happened? Does he actually not want to do what he's doing?" Were we in some awful game of chicken—was he waiting for me to beg him not to die? That had never occurred to me because he'd been so hell bent on doing it his way for so long. Should I try to change his mind?

But to what end? He'd grown increasingly frail. Was it right to try to convince him to live and bear it? Maybe so. I knew exactly what the priest and the nuns in that convent would have had to say about it. Then again, I also knew what *he* thought about it because he'd made his views clear to me for forty years. It's not unusual for the dying to become paranoid, and he had reason to be testy, his frustration fueled by impatience and unrealistic expectations. Still. I will never not wonder if I failed—if some part of him wanted to be coaxed to remain in the world. *Stay with me, Dad.*

Before he'd moved to hospice, I'd had an emergency Skype session with my therapist. She'd talked again about her theory (though she'd never met him) that Dad had a false face that he presented to the world, a persona he had clung to for so long that he'd lost a true sense of self-awareness. "But can somebody with a false face legitimately make the choice that he's making?" I asked. She thought about it and said she thought he could.

I studied her pixelated face on the screen. "I have to be very careful that I don't influence this chain of events. Because my life will be so much easier when he dies." There's the crux of it. I thought I'd been scrupulous, careful not to influence him. Now I was thrown into doubt. Guilt washes over me even now, cold creeping into my stomach, a swirling pattern: Why did the idea to stop eating embed in his brain?

The next morning he handed me a page from his journal, the only time he showed me what he'd written there.

"*Sunday 1-14-18. Last evening I offended Lauren and Genanne. I am sorry and deeply annoyed at myself. Slow to learn how to listen! Whatever came out I'm not sure, I remember feeling jumbled. I used some yahoo word that, I think, was misunderstood as suggesting that I thought they were scheming?? Farthest from my thought about either, especially since these days have been so bonding. Overnight, I have thought a lot about my not having really learned to hear what it is like to be taken for granted. And I realize how deeply and strongly you have determined to say: no more! Time to really honor the woman! I end smarter, I ~~hope~~ know.*"

I grabbed his hand, weeping as I read. It's all right, Dad. Of course it's all right.

We struggled on. The next morning he talked nonstop, rambling for more than an hour without a pause. He went round in circles, reciting the lineage of one wing of his large family: D begat E begat F. Q shot himself, R overdosed, S had a boat. It was difficult to witness, the compulsive recitation of a branch of the family that had scarcely given him the time of day—rich, conservative relations I'd always suspected made him feel, perhaps more than anyone in his sprawling Irish Catholic clan, unworthy. I wondered if he was having a panic attack. "Dad," I said, "you seem anxious, do you want to try something to calm you down?" He took a pill that the aide brought and went into a blissed-out daze for hours.

The next day he was fitful and cranky again, refusing drugs. He hadn't liked the fogginess, did not want to lose what consciousness he had left. "Of course," I told him. "You're driving the bus." He relayed with wonder that he'd dreamed he had dropped his iPod and broken it in the night, but on waking had found it nestled safe under his pillow. We kept talking and maybe I read to him, but I don't remember specifics.

And that, as it happens, was the last conversation we had.

His writing grows increasingly rickety, hard to read.

"*This a.m. I will try to stay in the Light and Prayer mode I experienced overnight. Today I'll try again to absorb the sense of "being" more at home with Oneness (or at least beginning).*

- *Interconnectedness*
- *No separation*
- *We are One united in that light* [unreadable]

The lost or broken iPod. After thinking all night that I heard it crash on the floor it is in the bed sheet! No separation! Today I accept my One—"

His final word, *oneness*, faded out, ink lightening to nothing. When I returned after lunch he was slouched in the wheelchair with the notebook and a blanket on his lap, his cheeks wet. I put my hand on his shoulder and spoke to him but he didn't respond. A nurse helped me get him into bed—he was light as a piece of balsam then, easy to maneuver.

Lauren was in D.C. Her mother was in the hospital with pneumonia. We thought she was dying on the east coast as my father was dying on the west coast, and we were riven, physically and emotionally—in ways I felt but did not fully grasp at the time. I was alone with Dad that final half week. Friends stepped in, met me for dinner nearby in the evenings. Alice brought more flowers, a pot of yellow daisies. I did not feel lonely. Or, no more lonely than usual. I sat and read to him. I took notes and lost them.

For the first time, he was silent. But he could clearly hear me—he turned his head as if listening and moved his arms and legs. He put one hand behind his neck and his right knee up, a reclining position so familiar, so completely *him*, I knew he was still aware, exerting his will. Somewhere in there he stood on a soapbox conducting his exit. Seeing his restlessness, one of the nurses told me chemicals are released during the final stages that can cause hallucinations or anxiety, a biological/chemical response. Worried that he was riddled with confusion or fear, I asked her to give him Haldol, feeling no compunction at all asking for it.

Later, when the fitfulness eased, a less familiar gesture: his arms raised like a conductor, slowly, gathering upward.

My father knew full well what happens to most people at the end of life. So many people who are in most ways far more practical, more reasonable than he are caught passive at the end, incapable of asserting their wishes. The man stopped eating—*he starved himself*—and he loved food! He lobbied his caregivers with such conviction, they let him have his way.

There was an element of Don Quixote in him. Deluded and good natured, committed to his own heroism, helping the helpless while embracing imagined glory. A protagonist who could never acknowledge his indebtedness to the humble, lesser beings who tramped along with him, clearing his path as best they could. "He's a legend in his own mind," he said once, mockingly, referring to some political pundit. This is a fairly accurate description of my father. He was the hero of his own story—artlessly committed to his vision, so earnest and truehearted and enamored of his tall tale that at key moments of his chaotic life, he carried others along with him.

My mother was a far better, more willing Sancho Panza than my grudging, exhausted, thin-skinned, guilty, paranoid, shell shocked self. And yet, I was there. I stood with him peering into the void. Even now, attempting to capture the experience, I fail. I can make myself look better than I was, or worse. The problem is, I was better *and* worse. I was everything. So was he. Cowardly, brave. Observant, clueless. Loving, petty. Strong, weak. And I felt, in those weeks, the largeness of it. Who can prepare for or explain it? I am not a religious person but I do understand the need for order when contemplating the wildness, the unpredictability, the vast mystery of one single human life. Oh, god: *help.*

My father was such an avid participant in his end that he created, for a time, an imprint on the system instead of the other way round. It reminds me of the Looney Tunes cartoons that play with false horizons, drawings created by one character meant to confuse another that instead become selectively permeable. A fake train tunnel painted on the side of a mountain, or a trompe l'oeil road that obscures a steep cliff. The coyote's complicated trick goes awry and the Road Runner barrels through the image and down the road, undeterred. In confusion and hope the coyote follows—

but the screen is a barrier now and he tears through, leaving a coyote-shaped cutout on the horizon.

My father painted a trompe l'oeil exit and burst through to his end with such gusto and determination, his outline still vibrates in the air.

Mourning is a kind of purgatory. You exist between worlds. For a long time I walked through, not fully feeling the world of the living or the world of the dead but aware of both.

On the night he died, I sat with him until about nine o'clock and then went home and fell into sleep. At 11:30 the nurse called to tell me he was gone. I dressed and walked through the dark streets and when I arrived the place was more hushed than usual, as if the building itself knew. He wore a clean white t-shirt and somebody had placed a yellow daisy between his folded hands. His face was a mask. I sat for a while with the body—it wasn't him—and then made my way home. We'd strung Christmas lights on the mantel and I sat on the floor in that magic light when the dogs came to greet me. There, nuzzled by two soft beasts, I did not weep.

I can grasp the scope of it only fleetingly, brief bursts that bloom and fade. A few months after his death I was at work, in an old building downtown. The single bathroom on each floor is on the stair landing, outside a heavy door. Doors on other landings slam open and shut, above and below, and the fluorescent light and dingy gray stairwell make it a place you don't want to dwell in for long. Walking out of the bathroom one day, I paused on the landing before pushing open the door to return to my desk. And there, in that functional, transitory space, the full labor of his death come over me, from a perspective not fully my own: how heavy and hard, how solitary.

He did it, he crossed over. I could never do it. And yet, I will.

The world is quick to sneer at idealists. They're easy marks, people who choose not to (or cannot) operate within the narrow tracks allotted to us here in the bumpy first quarter of what's shaping up to be a brutal century. All the qualities I longed for in a father when I was young—stability, practicality, reassurance—he couldn't deliver on most of them. But this set me free to meet him on even ground at the end. We were spirits on a journey, together for a time.

My wife and I went to the Mendocino Coast on Father's Day and scattered his ashes in the redwoods. I picked a spot in a tree circle and scattered the ash—so much more weighty and voluminous than you'd think—and read a Mary Oliver poem that he loved. It was peaceful and green and cool. But afterward, I was gripped by a fear of abandoning him, as if it were actually *him* in a bodily sense there under the trees. I had the strongest, most unsettling fear that my father would be cold there, that at night the dark would rush down from the trees, and when the river swelled its banks in winter he would feel the water closing over him. Being without the weight of him flicked a primal switch, and I could only grasp what had happened in a fixed, corporeal sense. Poems and comforting stories about spirit and atoms meant nothing. It was his body I fretted over, a body that by then had been dead—ash—for months. For the first time, I understood the appeal of a columbarium or a vase on the mantel, a climate-controlled container.

These feelings fleeted through me, wringing me out, and passed within a few days. I don't know if they passed because I overcame them or if they passed because I couldn't bear them. We left him there in the forest and drove away, a splitting that reverberates still.

At some point writing these notes, I had a hard time recording the correct year on the notebook paper. My hand wanted to write 1991—which is the year I left (or imagined I left) my parents behind and moved to San Francisco to begin a new, better life. Twenty years later, in 2011, Dad was living downstairs and the StoryCorps organization arrived in San Francisco with a mobile recording booth. The public was invited to come and record a conversation with a loved one—I'd heard excerpts on the radio and admired the honest, intimate conversations. I made an appointment and when the day came Dad and I rode the train downtown to the Contemporary Jewish Museum and sat for an hour together in a darkly lit recording booth with a volunteer moderator, talking. On listening now for the first time since we recorded it, the conversation sounds free flowing, organic. I asked Dad about his youth; he remembered few details about childhood other than the shock of his father's "complete nervous breakdown" and years-long stint at a sanitorium upstate (alcoholism, depression, the Depression). He spoke eloquently of his desire to enter the ministry as an impulse to "help others to understand their own best path," of his belief in catholicism with a small "c"—meaning universal.

I was interested, and the moderator was, too, in the love story. How had my parents come to disclose their feelings back when he was a priest, and how had he proposed? I asked about the timing when Mom became pregnant—this was why they left New York and finally married, right? No, he said, he wasn't a priest then. Well, maybe he *was* technically. He was still wearing a collar but had written a letter to Rome, resigning. (Here he pounds the table, speaking emphatically about the failures of Vatican Two.) But *you*, Dad, when did you decide to leave? He left in May, joining Mom in Virginia, where I was born five months later. Asked for details about my mother, he repeated what others had said about her. She was "self-effacing, laid back, quiet, genuine." But little else. "I do *regret* not having been more sensitive to listening to her and her views on things because as I said she was laid back, quiet, supportive..." He recalled visiting a neighbor who had been Mom's friend in her final years. The woman told him that once Mom came over for coffee and vented, saying, *I love him dearly but sometimes he drives me nuts*. This tidbit had stuck with him. A new perspective, something he'd never heard before: a belated understanding that he may have been a difficult person to live with. (Reader, he was). He trailed off. Relaying more specifics about my mother, the partner at his side for three decades—was beyond him. A love story with ample drama and yet so nonspecific it was confusing. Did he just not notice her that much? Or was he trying to protect their privacy? Maybe it was both.

"I probably was too authoritarian and directive when you were a kid," he ruminates at one point. Then, "I have a mental picture of you walking around the corner to school, wearing a poncho grandma had knitted, your hair in a ponytail. You were a very happy child. Your bubbliness—" I interrupted, objecting to that descriptive (no one I know would call me bubbly), and he backtracked, citing my "good disposition and graciousness." This struck me as a projection of vague girlish virtues. But I can hear now how important it was to him that I be happy because he'd been such an unhappy kid, a boy who watched his father leave the house on a stretcher and return in misery. And happiness is no small feat—not for him, not for anyone.

Another impression on listening to the CD: we sound as if we genuinely love each other. We're on our best behavior, yes, recording for posterity. But we sound like a nice duo enjoying each other's company—and suddenly I understand why the hospital nurses liked us. He had a lovely voice, truly, and could have been a radio announcer or a voice actor. Such a rich timbre on that plush, high quality recording, his voice and mine— sounding as if we are here together now, talking now.

Nothing's linear—time ripples in concentric circles and we stumble through, conflating years, bearing all of our selves within us. At the same time (how can this be?) he is gone from me, irrecoverable. Save for a recorded voice, some photos, his notebooks.

All my life I could count on two things from my father: love and upheaval. I felt acutely when he was dying that it was my destiny to walk that road with him—and for a time I grasped how our best selves met and our worst selves met and the wholeness of it was the thing. A giant wheel rose up where before there had been singular, hard spokes—this story or that, this disappointment or that shortcoming—the spokes still there but now part of something vast, spherical, apiece with some fundamental mystery.

I've lost that feeling now, but at least I can remember feeling it.

I'm struggling to make meaning, find a shape—but each paragraph closes off something true and immeasurable. I wanted him not to suffer. I wanted to exchange forgiveness. I wanted to help him. I wanted help. I wanted him to die, *to die*. Is my version fallible? Of course it is. I can glimpse an aspect of his journey and then a curtain falls and I'm pondering something utterly pedestrian. What to make for dinner? Some dish Dad would like—and he loved it all. Whatever I made, he'd take a bite, sigh, and proclaim his highest praise: "What an interesting combination of flavors!"

We'd talked about the upcoming second annual Women's March. "What would you write on a sign?" I asked. His answer was idealistic and spiritual and a little barmy and I carried it down Market Street with thousands of other marchers two days after he died, written in large red and black block letters. On the reverse side of the cardboard I wrote a slogan of my own, something deemed clever and relevant—but those words, whatever they were, have faded. It's his dream I remember: *UNIVERSAL ONENESS NOW*.

I don't want to be the main holder of his memory. I don't want to, but I am. I'll forget, I'll misconstrue. I will fail. Most days, I feel unequal to the task: A tiny flame against the obliterating void of impermanence. No wonder people build mausoleums. No wonder we hang our hopes on pearly gates. He didn't believe in pearly gates, but he believed his spirit would continue: stardust, essence, universal oneness. Sometimes I can meet him there in that belief. In some ways, my relationship with him continues to evolve. In some ways, we're on better footing now that he's dead. I know, on some days, that this sounds delusional.

I feel him more than I ever thought I would. His spirit, I mean. We've grown in understanding, Dad and me. Still talking together in the darkness— broader than broad, deeper than deep.

And that feeling, that hunch—that's my inheritance.

ACKNOWLEDGMENTS

I'm lucky and grateful that this essay found a home with WTAW Press. Thank you, Peg Alford Pursell, for everything.

These writers offered crucial insights and support along the way: Audrey Ferber, Anna Mantzaris, Rick May, Alice Templeton, Robert Thomas, Tracy Winn, Rebecca Winterer.

The end-of-life caregivers who give help and succor are essential in every sense.

Lauren Whittemore brings the light.

Thank you all.

Photo: Laura Duldner

Genanne Walsh is the author of *Twister*, awarded the Big Moose Prize for the Novel from Black Lawrence Press. Her work has appeared in *Puerto del Sol*, *Blackbird*, and elsewhere, and has been nominated for the Pushcart Prize. After thirty years in San Francisco she recently moved to Portland, Maine with her wife and dog. She's at work on a new novel.

Printed in the USA
CPSIA information can be obtained
at www.ICGtesting.com
JSHW022032291023
50974JS00012B/176